WOOF! WOOF! BARK! BARK!

GERMAN SHEPHERD DOG

Book For Kids
Children's Dog Books

petsunchained
(PETS & ANIMALS)

Speedy Publishing LLC
40 E. Main St. #1156
Newark, DE 19711
www.speedypublishing.com
Copyright 2017

In this book, we're going to talk all about German Shepherd dogs. So, let's get right to it!

German Shepherd dogs are one of the most popular breeds of dogs in America and worldwide. They were established as a breed in 1899. They are intelligent, loyal, and protective.

HISTORY OF THE GERMAN SHEPHERD

A captain in the German cavalry named Max von Stephanitz is responsible for the German Shepherd breed of dog that we know today. He worked for thirty-five years to breed the dog in a specific way. His goal was to develop a dog that was worthy of working with soldiers and policemen.

Originally, German Shepherds worked to herd sheep on ranches and farms. Their job was to protect large groups of sheep from predators, such as wolves. However, over time, the demand for dogs to serve this function decreased. This was when Max von Stephanitz began working to breed the German Shepherd to become an excellent guard dog with great stamina and intelligence.

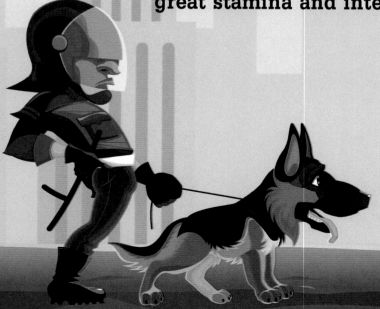

The Phylax Society, which was the first club dedicated to dog breeding, was established in Germany in the late 1800s. Max and other German Shepherd enthusiasts started the club. They wanted to standardize German Shepherds throughout the country. After this club was no longer operating, Max set up a society dedicated to the German Shepherd and used his own dog, called Horand von Grafrath, to breed a strong line of German Shepherds, the ancestors of today's breed.

During World War I, Max persuaded the police force in Germany to begin using German Shepherds in their work. Today, German Shepherds are used throughout the world by police and military organizations.

Because of their superior sense of smell, they can be trained to discover drugs and bombs. They are also used in search and rescue efforts to find people who are trapped in collapsed buildings.

TYPES OF GERMAN SHEPHERDS

There are several different types of German Shepherd dogs. They each have their own history and specific traits even though they are part of the same breed.

West German Show Lines

American and Canadian Show Lines

West German Working Lines

East German Working Lines

Czech Working Lines

Although these dogs are all German Shepherds, there is a big difference between the working lines and the show lines.

WORKING LINES

Working lines are not bred for specific looks, uniform coat colors, or a specific type of walk as show lines are. The breeders who develop working lines look for the qualities that Max von Stephanitz bred into the line:

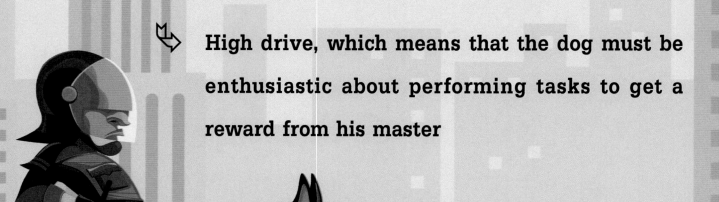

➪ High drive, which means that the dog must be enthusiastic about performing tasks to get a reward from his master

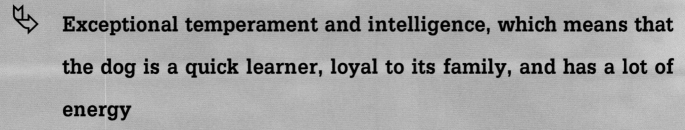 Exceptional temperament and intelligence, which means that the dog is a quick learner, loyal to its family, and has a lot of energy

Calm nerves, which means that the dog can be confident when threats are present, such as sirens or gunshots

Physical features, which for working dogs means an agile and compact body with short-haired coats of different colors

SHOW LINES

Show lines of German Shepherds have been bred to win competitions and to become family pets. They differ from working lines in the following ways:

→ A lower level of drive than the working line

→ Longer, thicker coats that have more uniform colors, usually red and black or tan and black with the black saddle shape on their backs

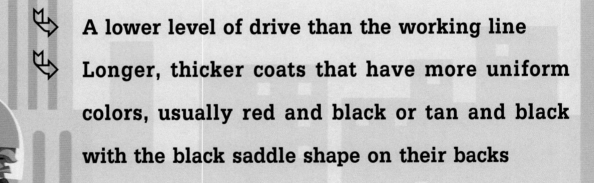

Bigger, bulkier bodies than the working lines

Personality and demeanor to become good pets, but only when raised appropriately

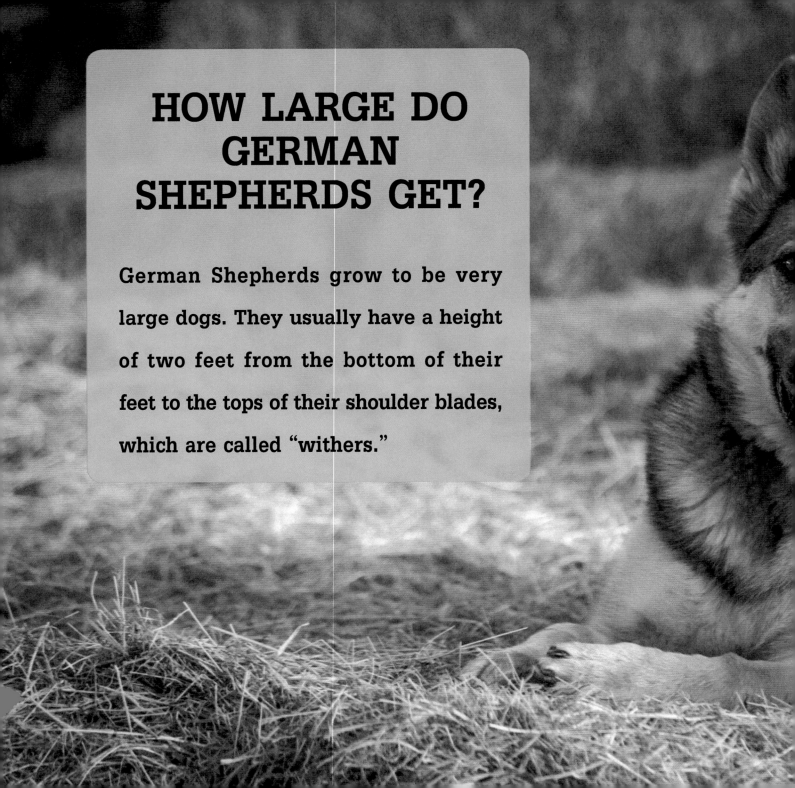

HOW LARGE DO GERMAN SHEPHERDS GET?

German Shepherds grow to be very large dogs. They usually have a height of two feet from the bottom of their feet to the tops of their shoulder blades, which are called "withers."

An adult German Shepherd weighs from 50 pounds to as much as 90 pounds or more. They have long, bushy tails and tall pointy ears.

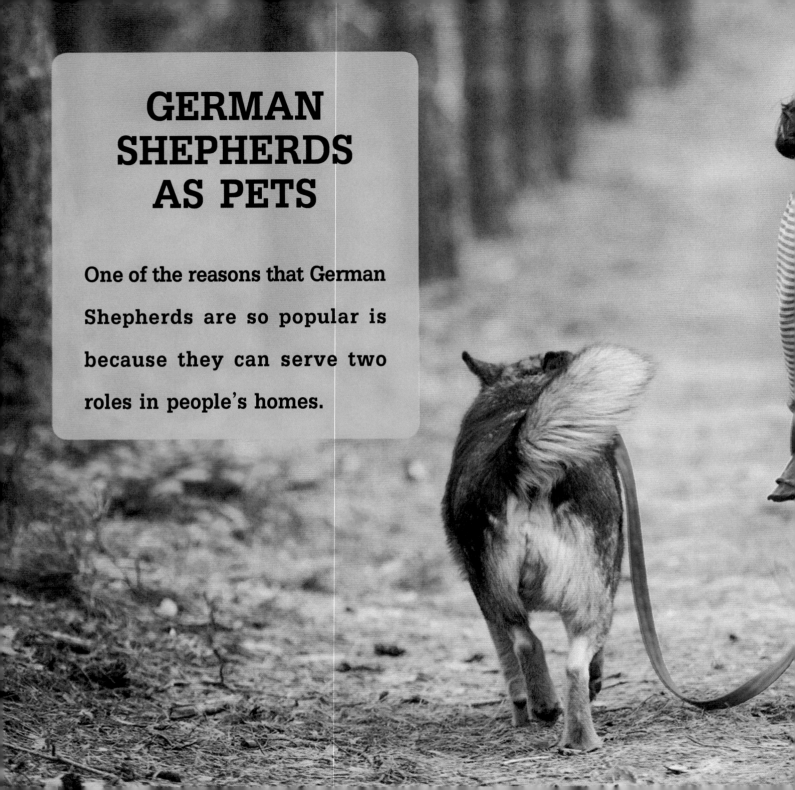

GERMAN SHEPHERDS AS PETS

One of the reasons that German Shepherds are so popular is because they can serve two roles in people's homes.

They can guard the family home because they are alert to danger. They're also good pets because they are obedient as well as intelligent. In addition, they'll do whatever they can to make the family they live with happy.

They need to have regular exercise and they are highly active. They perform well in competitions that show their athletic ability. Because they are so intelligent, they need mental stimulation too. Sometimes, if not trained properly, they can be too protective of their families and unfriendly to outsiders. It sometimes takes them a while to become friendly with a new person.

THE GERMAN SHEPHERD COAT

The coats of German Shepherds come in many different combinations of colors. Some are even all black. Their coat has two layers in order to help insulate them from cold. Their outer layer sheds throughout the year. Most German Shepherds have hair of medium length, but there's also a type that's been recognized that has longer hair.

ADVANTAGES AND DISADVANTAGES OF THE GERMAN SHEPHERD BREED

No matter how superior a dog breed is, every breed has advantages and disadvantages.

Most German Shepherds are quick learners because they're so intelligent. They are considered to be the third most intelligent dog after collies and poodles. However, the person who trains the German Shepherd must be firm as well as gentle.

The reason for this is because it needs to be made clear that the person who is the head of the family is the "alpha dog." The German Shepherd must obey the commands of this master otherwise the dog might try to become dominant, which leads to behavior problems.

Because this type of calm, careful training is essential to having a good family pet, German Shepherds are not the easiest choice for a first-time dog owner. However, for a family who knows how to train the German Shepherd when it is a puppy, it can become a valued member of the family.

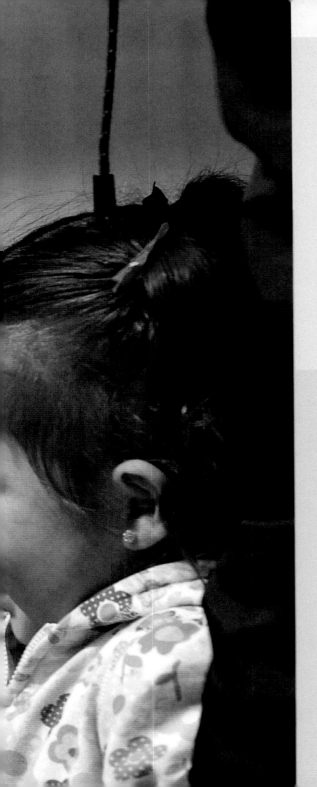

These dogs are loyal and protective of all family members and are good with children. They do grow to be large dogs so if there are babies or toddlers in the house, supervision will be needed.

They need a large yard or area to run around and shouldn't be living in tight spaces since they need at least two hours of exercise every day. Sometimes they can have health disorders that require expensive veterinary treatments.

They also need lots of activities to keep them mentally stimulated, otherwise they sometimes act out by becoming noisy or destructive. These types of behavior happen because they feel neglected or they're bored. They really thrive on the company of people and get unhappy when they are left alone for any length of time.

HEALTH RISKS FOR GERMAN SHEPHERDS

German Shepherds generally live for about 10 to 12 years. They have a tendency to develop infections in their ears.

They also frequently have problems with their hips and sometimes their elbows as they age.

FAMOUS GERMAN SHEPHERDS

There have been many famous German Shepherds. Here are two of the most famous.

STRONGHEART

Etzel von Oeringen, known on screen as Strongheart, was born in 1917 and became one of the first dog film stars.

He was trained to be a police dog in Germany and was brought to the United States when he was three years old.

Laurence Trimble, who was an animal trainer as well as a director, and his wife Jane Murfin, who was a screenwriter, looked for a dog that could act in motion pictures. When Trimble found Etzel in 1920, he knew that he had found what he was looking for. However, Etzel, now known as Strongheart, had to be socialized before he could appear in a movie.

Trimble kept him by his side all day and all night and retrained him. Strongheart eventually lost the aggressiveness that he needed to be a police dog, although he was able to detect criminals and would still chase after them. He appeared in six films and has a star on the Hollywood Walk of Fame. His line survives today.

RIN TIN TIN

During World War I, an American soldier by the name of Lee Duncan found an abandoned dog kennel on the battlefield. He rescued a German Shepherd puppy and brought him back to California with him when he went home. During his childhood, Duncan had lived in an orphanage for five years. When his mother came back to get him he lived with his grandparents and there was no one to play with him so he got a dog. As an adult, Duncan became attached to the cute pup as soon as he saw him.

He knew he had to take the pup home with him. He called him Rinty. They became friends and Duncan found a way to get Rinty into the movies where he was known as Rin Tin Tin. Rin Tin Tin became very famous and was an actor in many different movies. Just like Strongheart, Rin Tin Tin has a star on the Walk of Fame.

GERMAN SHEPHERDS ARE EXCEPTIONAL GUARD DOGS

German Shepherds are exceptional guard dogs and they can be wonderful family pets if they are trained properly as puppies. Because of their intelligence, strength, stamina, and extraordinary ability to smell, German Shepherds are frequently used by police and military organizations, as well as search and rescue teams.

Awesome! Now that you've read German Shepherds you may want to read facts about cats in the Pets Unchained book Here Kitty! Kitty! | Fun Facts Cats Book for Kids | Children's Cat Books.

Made in the USA
Middletown, DE
21 December 2021